Sailboats
Flagpoles
Cranes

Sailboats
Flagpoles
Cranes

USING PULLEYS AS
SIMPLE
MACHINES

BY CHRISTOPHER LAMPTON
PICTURES BY CAROL NICKLAUS

THE MILLBROOK PRESS · BROOKFIELD, CT.
A GATEWAY BOOK

Library of Congress Cataloging-in-Publication Data

Lampton, Christopher

Sailboats, flagpoles, cranes: using pulleys as simple
machines/by Christopher Lampton: pictures by Carol Nicklaus
p.   cm.
Includes index
Summary: Examines simple machines that are actually
pulleys, including flagpoles, cranes, and the pulleys on a sailboat.
ISBN 1-56294-026-0
1. Simple Machines—Juvenile literature.   2. Pulleys—
Juvenile literature.   [1. Pulleys.   2. Simple machines.]
I. Nicklaus, Carol, ill.   II. Title.
TJ147.L283   1991
621.8'11—dc20   91-19583 CIP AC

Have you ever wondered why we pull on a string to raise and lower venetian blinds? Have you ever raised a flag on a pole by pulling down on a rope that stretches from the top of the flagpole to the bottom? Why do you think we use this rope?

Because it's easier, that's why! You could raise your blinds without the help of the string, but you'd have to use a chair or ladder to reach the top of the window. And pulling on a rope to raise and lower the flag sure beats climbing to the top of the pole!

In both cases you've used a **pulley** to help you do work. You may not think of a pulley as a machine, but it definitely is. A pulley is what we call a **simple machine.** There are three other kinds of simple machines: the lever, the wheel and axle, and the inclined plane.

Complex machines are made up of combinations of simple machines. When you think of machines, you probably think of complex machines—airplanes, washing machines, and cars, for example. But hidden inside complex machines are simple machines, and the pulley is one of them.

Machines need energy to do work. Many complex machines are powered by electricity or gasoline. But when you use a simple machine, you often have to use some muscle power yourself. A shovel, for instance, is a simple machine for moving dirt. As you know, you have to lift the shovel with your arms to move a load of dirt. And when you raise the blinds or lower the flag, you also apply effort to get the job done.

Why would you use a simple machine if you still have to do work? Because a simple machine can make your work easier. How is this so?

To answer this question we first need to define work. Scientists have a special way of defining it. They measure how much force you use to move something and the distance over which you apply this force. Then, they multiply the force that you use times the distance that you move something to measure how much work is done. In other words, **Force $\times$ Distance = Work.**

This means that the amount of work you do to move something depends on how much effort you put in over a certain distance. But it also means that you can make the amount of force smaller as long as you make the distance greater.

You can choose to apply less force over a greater distance or more force over less distance, depending on which makes the job easier. But you'll still be doing the same amount of work! We call this a **trade-off** because we either trade distance for force or force for distance.

Now let's make a pulley to see what kind of an advantage it can give you when you do work.

There are several different kinds of pulleys, so first we need to decide which kind we're going to make. A pulley usually consists of a wheel with a rope running over it. When the rope moves, the wheel turns with it. The wheel has a groove along its rim so the rope won't slip off. This type of wheel is known as a **sheave.**

You can hang a pulley above the ground from a hook or bar and use the rope to lift things. This kind of pulley is called a **fixed pulley** because, even though the sheave turns, the pulley stays in one place.

It's easy to make a fixed pulley of your own. You'll need a rope (a white clothesline would be best) about 20 feet long. Ask someone to remove some clothes from a closet until a section of the crossbar is empty. Drape the rope over the bar so that some of it is hanging down on either side. There's your pulley!

You might wonder where the wheel is. Most pulleys use wheels because they reduce friction as the rope moves over them. When a pulley doesn't have a wheel, the rope rubs as it moves. This both slows it down and wears it out. Still, it's possible to make a pulley—such as the one you've just made—without a wheel. Instead, the crossbar plays the role of the wheel.

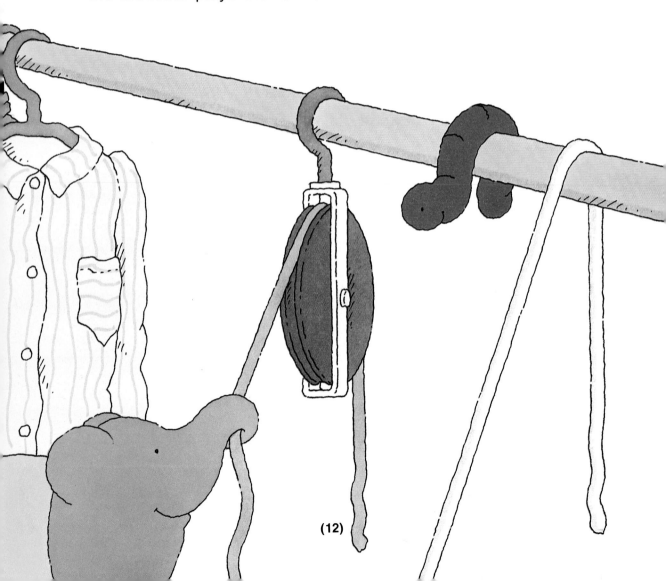

Now you need something to lift with your pulley.
Find an empty container with a built-in handle, such as
the kind used to hold milk, juice, or laundry detergent.
Fill it half-full with water and screw the lid on tight so
nothing spills out when you're doing the experiment. Tie
one end of the rope firmly around the handle of the
container and pull down on the loose end of the rope
that is hanging over the crossbar.

You've just used a fixed pulley to lift a weight. We call this weight the **load.**

Unfortunately, a fixed pulley alone does not allow us to trade off force for distance. It takes just as much effort to lift the load with a single fixed pulley as it does to lift the load directly.

You do gain an advantage, though. When you pull down on the rope to lift the container, your effort seems less because you use the weight of your body to help you. When you lift the container with your hands, some of the weight of your body must be lifted too. Even though the amount of lifting force is really the same, it's easier for you to pull down than to lift up.

The fixed pulley has given you what is known as a **change in direction.** You get this same advantage in the case of the flagpole and the blinds.

If you want to make a trade-off, you'll need to add a second kind of pulley, called a **movable pulley,** to your fixed pulley. Here's how you do it.

Untie the rope from the handle of the container. Then, feed the rope through the handle and tie the end of the rope to the crossbar. The handle of the container is now your movable pulley. Pull down on the loose end of the rope until the container lifts off the floor. The rope should slide through the handle and over the closet bar.

You probably noticed that by adding the movable pulley you reduced the effort you used to move your load, and you also pulled more rope through the handle. In other words, you used a movable pulley to trade force for distance.

And don't forget that when you add a movable pulley to a fixed pulley, you also gain the advantage from the fixed pulley's change of direction! If you want to, you can do without the fixed pulley altogether by lifting the container with the section of rope between the handle and the crossbar. But let's face it, most of us choose to use every advantage we've got!

Now that you're convinced that the movable pulley gives you a trade-off, let's measure the distances to figure out how much of a trade-off you get. You'll need to compare how far up you lift the load and how much rope you use to lift it.

Find a yardstick and a felt-tipped pen. Use the movable pulley to lift your load a little way off the floor. Now, with your free hand, make a mark where the rope crosses the bar.

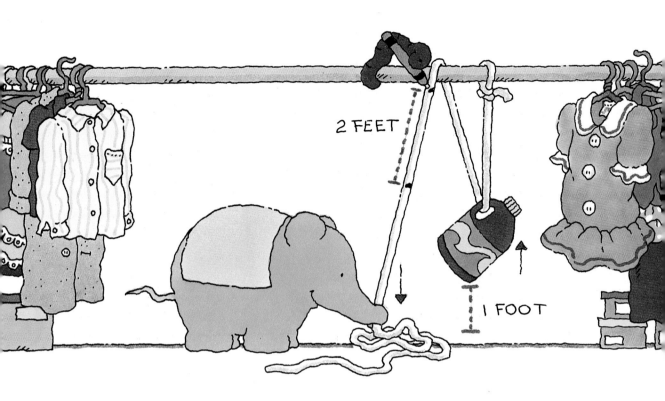

2 FEET

1 FOOT

Then, pull down on the rope to lift the container about 1 foot higher. Mark where the rope now crosses the bar.

Now measure the distance between the two marks. You should find that you pulled the rope down about 2 feet—twice as far as the container moved up. Using the movable pulley, you needed less effort—about ½ as much as without it. You used ½ the force to lift the load, but you had to pull the rope down twice as far.

When a machine lets you trade off force for distance or distance for force, we say that it has given you a **mechanical advantage.** The pulley allowed you to use ½ the force to lift the load. But you had to pull the rope down 2 feet in order to lift the load 1 foot. Using the movable pulley has given you a mechanical advantage of 2.

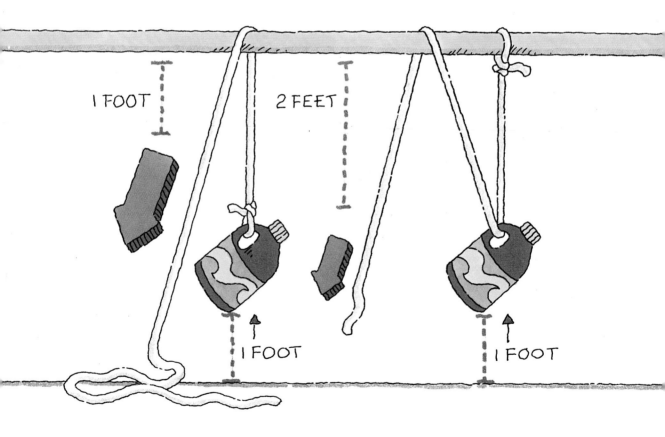

A quick way to find the mechanical advantage of a pulley is to count the sections of rope that are supporting the load. Remember your fixed pulley? How many sections of rope supported your load? Only 1, right? Well, a mechanical advantage of 1 means there is no advantage. The distance and the force remain the same. Without a trade-off, the fixed pulley doesn't actually reduce the effort needed to lift the load. (Although it does give you the advantage of a change in direction.)

You've just discovered that when there are 2 sections of rope supporting the weight of the load, the mechanical advantage is 2. But do you think it's possible for a pulley to cut the effort you use to lift a load by ¼? Yes, it is. Let's see how.

You'll need to put several pulleys together to make what is called a **block and tackle.** A block and tackle is a combination of several fixed and movable pulleys attached to one another.

Start with your movable pulley. Take the loose end of the rope and pass it through the handle of the container a second time. If you drape it over the bar a second time as well, you'll get the added advantage of a change in direction, just as before. (Remember, though, that the rope you pull down on is not helping to support the load!)

When you lift your load, notice how much rope you have used by the time it has risen only about 1 foot. You've used a lot, haven't you? But the load is much easier to lift this time. Can you guess how much less effort you've used? Just count the ropes that support your load!

4 FEET

DOWN

UP

1 FOOT

You had to pull the rope 4 times as far, but you only had to use ¼ the amount of force to lift the load, since the weight of the load was split between the 4 ropes. Or, in other words, you gained a mechanical advantage of 4.

It doesn't take much effort to lift a half-empty juice container, whether you use a pulley or not. But many times people have to move things that would be very hard or even impossible for them to move without the aid of a pulley.

On a sailboat, everywhere you look there are
pulleys! Fixed pulleys are used to raise the sails and to
control their movement in the wind. Pulleys make it
easier to haul in on ropes, called sheets, so that even
on a gusty day a sailor can control the sails.

Lots of complex machines depend on pulleys, too, such as elevators, oil derricks, tow trucks, and cranes, to name a few. They have very big engines to provide energy, but without the block and tackle they wouldn't be able to provide enough force to lift a crowd of people, or sections of pipe, or cars and trucks, or huge loads of cement blocks and steel girders.

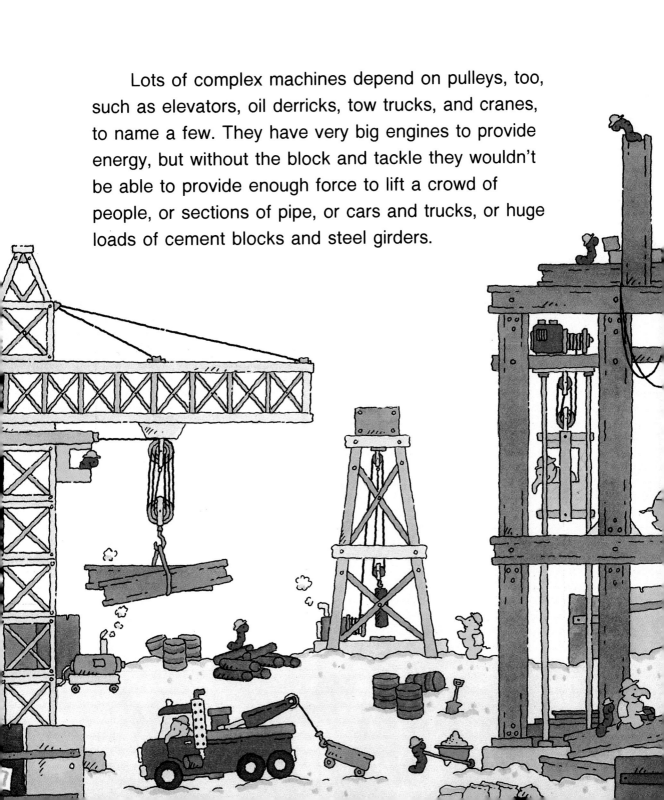

Can you figure out how much of a mechanical advantage this tow truck gains by using these pulleys? And the oil derrick? How about the elevator? And the crane?

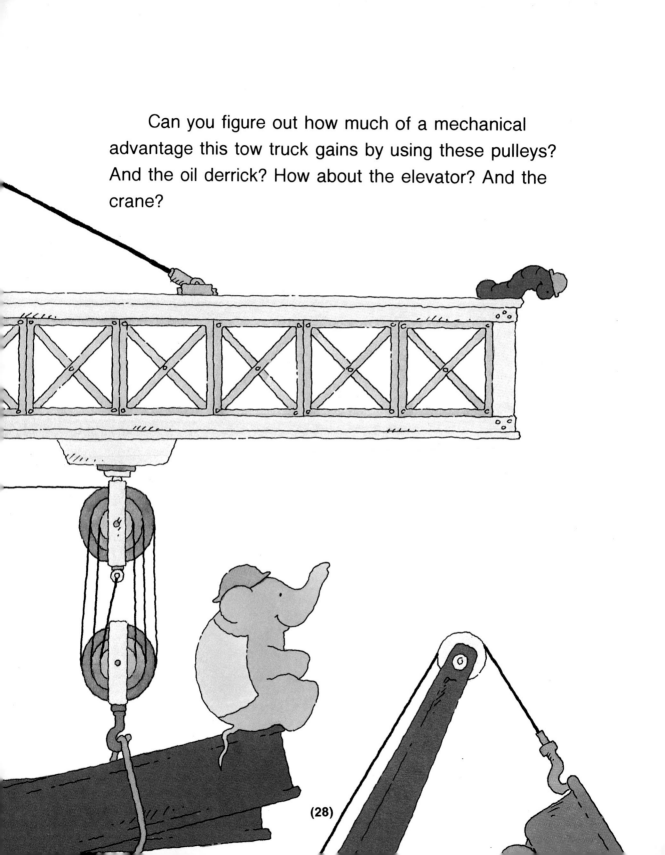

tow truck   1
elevator   4
oil derrick   2
crane   6

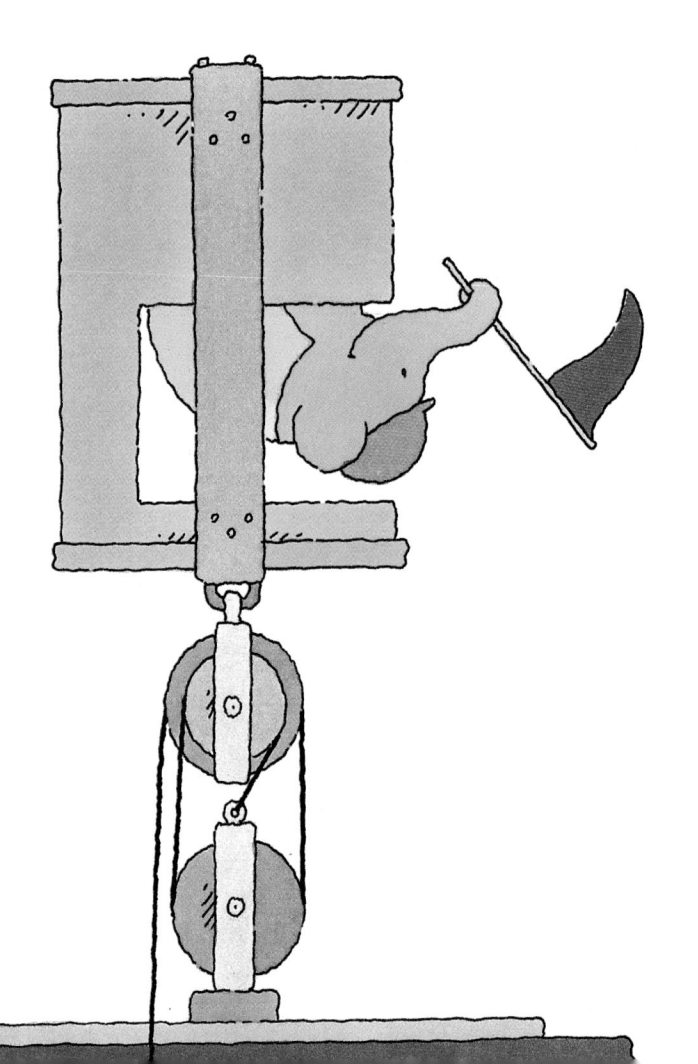

It would make sense if the word *pulley* came from the word *pull,* wouldn't it? But it doesn't. Actually, it comes from a Greek word meaning "axle." In ancient Greece, pulleys were often nothing more than a rope pulled around a piece of wood. The wood turned as an axle does inside a wheel.

Today, lots of pulleys turn around a wheel and axle. But the pulley that you made in your closet was all axle and no wheel. In that way, it was more like the pulleys made by people living thousands of years ago, the ones that gave pulleys their name.

Index / Glossary